ACCESS THE ACTION!

Scan the QR code to
hear this story for
FREE!

Published in the UK by Sweet Cherry Publishing Limited, 2025
Unit 4u18, The Book Brothers Business Park,
Tolwell Road, Leicester LE4 1BR, United Kingdom

Unit 31, The Pottery, Bakers Point,
Pottery Road, Dún Laoghaire,
Dublin A96 EV18, Ireland

SWEET CHERRY and associated logos are trademarks and/or registered trademarks of Sweet Cherry Publishing Limited.

2 4 6 8 10 9 7 5 3 1

ISBN: 978-1-80263-534-8

Football Rising Stars: Gianluigi Donnarumma

© Sweet Cherry Publishing Limited, 2025

Text by Steve George
Illustrations by Sophie Jones

All rights reserved. No part of this publication may be reproduced or utilised in any form or by any means, electronic or mechanical, including photocopying, recording, or using any information storage and retrieval system, without prior permission in writing from the publisher. No part of this publication may be used or reproduced in any manner for the purpose of training artificial intelligence technologies or systems.

The right of Steve George to be identified as the author of this work has been asserted by them in accordance with the Copyright, Designs and Patents Act 1988.

This book is not authorised, licensed or approved by Gianluigi Donnarumma. Any faults are the publisher's, who will be happy to rectify for future printings.

www.sweetcherrypublishing.com

Printed and bound in India

GIANLUIGI DONNARUMMA
THE UNOFFICIAL STORY

Written by

STEVE GEORGE

Sweet Cherry

CONTENTS

1. A Bad Start	7
2. A Born Goalkeeper	14
3. Through the Ranks	23
4. Number 99	29
5. Milan's Number One	37
6. Money Talks	48
7. The Two Gianluigis	54
8. A Disappointing Season	64
9. Goodbye, Milan	76
10. Road to the Final	86
11. Penalties	96
12. A New Start	107
13. Domestic Glory	117
14. What's Next?	124

1
A BAD START

On the 21st of May 2016, great rivals AC Milan and Juventus met in the final of the Coppa Italia – the annual domestic cup competition in the Italian leagues.

While Juventus were flying high, Milan were having yet another

★★ FOOTBALL RISING STARS ★★

disappointing year. The club was currently in its fifth trophyless season, and this was their first final since 2003. Determined to prove themselves, the players wanted to make the most of the opportunity and claim victory.

Milan dominated the majority of the game, creating chance after chance, but failed to find the back of the net. Juventus struggled to match the energy of Milan, and any chances they managed to carve out on goal were easily dealt

★ GIANLUIGI DONNARUMMA ★

with by Milan's seventeen-year-old goalkeeper, Gianluigi Donnarumma.

Gianluigi was having a remarkable first full season, performing well and already getting noticed in a struggling Milan team. Determined to do whatever it took to give his team the best chance possible of winning this final game, he'd been a force to be reckoned with in goal.

The score was still 0-0 at full time, so the match went into extra time. Both teams pushed for a goal but still couldn't find the back of the net.

In the second half of extra time, Álvaro Morata came off the bench for Juventus. On his first touch, he met a perfect flighted cross with a sublime half-volley that beat Gianluigi.

Gianluigi turned quickly and watched as the ball bounced across the back of his goal and nestled in the left-hand corner. Already on his knees after diving low to try to stop Morata's volley, the realisation that Juventus had scored hit him and he sank to the ground, his head in his hands in despair. In stark contrast, Morata and his teammates

★ GIANLUIGI DONNARUMMA ★

joyfully hurdled over the advertising boards and ran to celebrate with the screaming Juventus fans.

Being a goalkeeper is the toughest job in football, especially when the other team scores. Gianluigi had saved many goals throughout the match, but that wouldn't matter if Milan didn't find a way to equalise or win. It was difficult, but he found the strength to move on and refocus on the rest of the game.

In the last minute of injury time, Milan won a corner. Gianluigi ran the

 length of the pitch into Juventus' penalty area to join the attack in one last chance.

As the ball was whipped into the box, Gianluigi rose to meet it with thoughts of scoring an unlikely equaliser ... but it was too high. A scrambled clearance bobbled agonisingly close to him, falling instead to Milan defender José Mauri. Mauri's shot deflected off a Juventus player and missed the goal by inches. It was the last shot of the game, and Juventus had won.

★ GIANLUIGI DONNARUMMA ★

After the game, Gianluigi was upset and cried over the loss. All footballers hate to lose, but goalkeepers more so. To be scored against is a personal insult and all anyone will remember (or talk about) are your mistakes.

But Gianluigi also felt very optimistic. The defeat was difficult to accept, but he knew that he would get more opportunities to shine. After all, he was still young and his career was only just beginning.

2
A BORN GOALKEEPER

Gianluigi Donnarumma was born on the 25th of February 1999. His family lived in Castellammare di Stabia, a town in the Italian region of Naples. The town is only a few miles away from Pompeii, the ancient Roman city that was destroyed when the Mount

GIANLUIGI DONNARUMMA

Vesuvius volcano erupted thousands of years ago.

The Naples region has produced some of Italy's best strikers over the years. Many of them have gone into Serie A, the Italian first division, including top goalscorers Lorenzo Insigne, Antonio Di Natale and Ciro Immobile. Famous Italian striker Fabio Quagliarella was born in the same town as Gianluigi.

With all the goalscoring talent coming from Naples, it's probably no surprise that many great goalkeepers have also emerged from the region.

★ FOOTBALL RISING STARS ★

After all, they clearly get plenty of practice! Gianluigi may be the most well-known, but there are many others. Gennaro Iezzo, Antonio Mirante and Gianluigi's own brother, Antonio, have also all risen through the ranks at the local football club, ASD Club Napoli.

When Gianluigi was just four years old, his uncle – who was a goalkeeper himself – took him to ASD Club Napoli.

Gianluigi was born to be a goalkeeper. He was already tall for his

★ GIANLUIGI DONNARUMMA ★

age and had a natural ability. Every time his uncle took a shot, Gianluigi fearlessly dived down onto the hard, dry dirt pitch to save it. He quickly fell in love with football and would cry if it rained and he couldn't play.

During his time training at ASD Club Napoli, Gianluigi was able to learn a lot about being a good goalkeeper. While being tall and brave were both helpful, he knew those qualities alone wouldn't automatically make him a successful player.

★ FOOTBALL RISING STARS ★

Getting in the way of a ball flying towards you at seventy miles per hour is only half the job. Modern goalkeepers also have to be what is often referred to as a sweeper keeper, acting like an extra defender, pushing high up the pitch and assisting the team with starting attacks and maintaining possession. It's no longer about just standing on your line and waiting for the ball to come to you. Goalkeepers also need to be confident, concentrate hard, have accurate passing skills, make quick decisions and have the nerve to shout

★ GIANLUIGI DONNARUMMA ★

at defenders when they're not paying attention.

By the age of ten, Gianluigi was almost six foot tall. His mother had to bring his birth certificate to every match to prove he wasn't lying about his age!

At home, Gianluigi's bedroom walls were a shrine to famous goalkeepers. His idols were Italian international goalkeeper Gianluigi Buffon and Brazilian goalkeeper Dida. Another one of his favourites was someone a lot closer to home – his older brother, Antonio.

FOOTBALL RISING STARS

Antonio played for ASD Club Napoli, after also being introduced to the club by his uncle. He was then signed by Juve Stabia, a professional club who played in the Italian third division (Serie C), before joining top Italian side AC Milan at the age of fifteen. As soon as they signed his brother, Gianluigi became a huge fan of Milan and fell in love with the club.

Gianluigi himself was soon attracting attention from the big clubs in Italy. His coaches at ASD Club Napoli knew he was going to be a star and weren't shy about letting people know. The club's goalkeeping coach had already helped train several goalkeepers who had gone on to play in Serie A, and it was clear that Gianluigi had learnt from the best.

After impressing in a trial match, fourteen-year-old Gianluigi was approached by Inter Milan – AC Milan's neighbours. He was all set to join the club, but signing for the other Milan club didn't feel right.

At the last minute, AC Milan came to speak to Gianluigi and asked him to sign for them instead. It was an easy decision. Gianluigi wanted to follow in his brother's footsteps and join the club he supported.

And so, despite being on the verge of joining Inter Milan, Gianluigi signed for AC Milan instead.

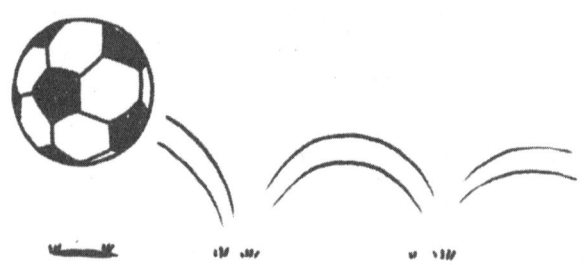

3

THROUGH THE RANKS

Moving to the nation's capital city to join the youth team at AC Milan wasn't easy for young Gianluigi. Homesickness set in quickly, and while playing video games with his new teammates helped, being so far from home was very difficult for him.

★ FOOTBALL RISING STARS ★

One place Gianluigi always felt at home was on the pitch. He settled into his role quickly, playing in the age group above his own where he still towered over the other players. Like his coaches at ASD Club Napoli, the youth coaches at Milan knew he was something special – a one-in-a-million prospect.

His impressive performances at youth level continued as he rose through the ranks, and he received an unbelievable early birthday present three days before he was due to turn sixteen: a place on the Milan first team bench. The club had to get special medical permission to confirm that Gianluigi could play with adults, despite his now six-foot-five frame.

The Milan manager at the time, Filippo Inzaghi, knew he was on borrowed time because the team weren't doing well. He considered giving Gianluigi his full debut on the last game of the season, thinking that a win, lose or draw didn't matter, but he decided against it. Inzaghi desperately hoped that a win might save his job for the next season. Milan won the match, but Inzaghi didn't get to keep his job.

The next manager, Siniša Mihajlović, was also a fan of Gianluigi. He gave him a debut during a pre-season tour of China in a match against Real Madrid, replacing first team goalkeeper Diego López in the 72nd minute.

Mihajlović was reluctant to play Gianluigi when the new season started, but he soon realised that a drastic change was

GIANLUIGI DONNARUMMA

needed. After just eight games, Milan was eleventh in the league and had conceded fourteen goals. Their first-choice goalkeeper, López, was struggling, so the Milan manager had a decision to make.

He asked Christian Abbiati, an experienced keeper in his final season and about to retire, if he thought Gianluigi was ready to take the step up. Having trained alongside Gianluigi, Abbiati knew exactly what the young goalkeeper was all about. Without hesitation, his answer to

Mihajlović's question was a big yes.

The day before Milan's next game, Gianluigi sat down with the manager and was told he would be making his Serie A debut. When asked if he was afraid to play, the fearless Gianluigi replied no. But while he was not nervous, it was still an emotional moment for him – an opportunity he didn't think would happen so soon.

He rushed home after training and excitedly told his parents to get on a train and come to Milan, because he was starting the game tomorrow.

4
NUMBER 99

On the 25th of October 2015, Gianluigi made his competitive debut for Milan in a game against Sassuolo. He was sixteen years and 242 days old, making him the second youngest goalkeeper to ever play in Serie A.

While he stood in the tunnel, waiting to walk onto the pitch, the butterflies were starting to flutter a little in Gianluigi's stomach. What was happening hadn't really sunk in yet, but he felt more than ready to show the fans what he could do.

After the lineup, Gianluigi ran over to his goal. Wearing the number 99 shirt (picked because 1999 was the year he was born), he touched his crossbar and got ready to play.

It's fair to say that his debut wasn't a roaring success. The opponents, Sassuolo, weren't having the best of starts to the season themselves and were not exactly scoring for fun either.

★ GIANLUIGI DONNARUMMA ★

Gianluigi's first real test was a long-range shot that bounced in front of him. It could have caused a problem, but he tracked the ball well and caught it easily.

He was his usual fearless self throughout the match, jumping into crowds of players for high balls and even diving at an advancing opposition player's feet when he was put through on goal.

Milan took the lead through a penalty, but Sassuolo equalised with an excellent free kick that beat Gianluigi at his near post. A late goal in the 86th minute gave Milan the lead again, and they held on to win 2-1.

Although he had won his debut game, Gianluigi was still upset about conceding a goal – despite it being a free kick most goalkeepers would have struggled to save. But, as we know, goalkeepers hate to be scored against no matter the overall result.

It wasn't the worst debut, and Gianluigi had done everything he could. At least he didn't get sent off after three minutes or concede

GIANLUIGI DONNARUMMA

thirteen goals. Most importantly, he didn't look out of place on the pitch and received good reviews. He had done enough to prove his manager's confidence in him and keep his place in the side.

In his next appearance, he kept a clean sheet in a win against Chievo. This was followed by a win against Lazio, but he was unable to keep another clean sheet in that match.

Gianluigi was starting to get noticed across the country, but it was in the next game against Atalanta when he showed exactly what he could do.

In the 63rd minute, a point-blank header from an Atalanta striker landed just in front of Gianluigi. Reacting quickly, Gianluigi dropped to the ground and pushed the ball away, saving what looked like a certain goal.

Not even a minute later, Gianluigi saved another strong close-range shot, turning it around the post after the Milan defence were caught napping. A little annoyed, Gianluigi suggested that his teammates pay closer attention to the game.

Milan had started to turn their season around, helped by the growing

GIANLUIGI DONNARUMMA

confidence of their young goalkeeper. Gianluigi would go on to make thirty-one appearances for Milan, keeping eleven clean sheets. One of them was in the big derby 3-0 win against Inter Milan.

After the final game of the season, retiring goalkeeper Abbiati took Gianluigi's arm and raised it in a baton-passing moment. Abbiati had become a mentor to Gianluigi, so the gesture meant a lot to him and even made him cry.

★✦ **FOOTBALL RISING STARS** ✦★

Gianluigi was now a firm favourite amongst the AC Milan fans and was getting praise from all over. Italy's leading sports paper, *La Gazzetta dello Sport*, said that he was the only reason to smile in a tortuous season.

The 2015/2016 season ended with the heartbreak of losing the Coppa Italia final against Juventus, but things were looking up for Milan and for Gianluigi. They were going into the new season full of confidence and with some hope that it would be much better than the one before.

5
MILAN'S NUMBER ONE

In the opening game of the 2016/2017 Serie A season, Milan were playing at home against Torino. Milan were comfortably winning 3-1 by the 90th minute, but then a Torino goal made the score 3-2 and put Milan and their fans on edge.

★ **FOOTBALL RISING STARS** ★

Deep into injury time, nerves got a lot worse when Milan defender Gabriel Paletta conceded a penalty and got himself sent off for his second yellow card.

In the lead-up to the actual penalty, Gianluigi paced at the back of his goal while the Milan and Torino players prepared themselves, each team trying to put the other one off. Finally, the ball was placed on the spot.

Torino's Andrea Belotti took the responsibility and stepped up to take the penalty. Approaching the ball with

a little shimmy, he blasted it low – but Gianluigi had already figured out where Belotti was going to put it and dived the right way, knocking the ball away.

Gianluigi had just saved the first penalty of his professional career! Thanks to him, Milan held onto their lead and won 3-2.

Now firmly in place as the number one goalkeeper for Milan, Gianluigi kept his first clean sheet of the season a few games later in a 1-0 victory against Sampdoria, followed up by two more clean sheets against Lazio and Fiorentina.

★ FOOTBALL RISING STARS ★

The highlight of the season came in the 2016 Supercoppa Italiana final, a one-off game between the previous season's Serie A winners and Coppa Italia winners. Because Juventus had won both competitions, this gave Milan as the Coppa Italia runners up a chance to get revenge for the cup final defeat.

Gianluigi was called into action early, tipping the ball over the bar from a half-volley shot. He saved a couple more efforts, but then Juventus opened the scoring from a corner in the 18th minute. Despite

★ GIANLUIGI DONNARUMMA ★

a full-stretch dive, Gianluigi was powerless to stop the well-hit volley.

Up until this point, Milan had been struggling to get into the game. However, they managed to push back and score an equaliser not long before half-time.

Milan continued to dominate the game in the second half and nearly scored, hitting the crossbar. In the 67th minute, a long-range shot from Juventus midfielder Sami Khedira was heading for the top corner, but Gianluigi made a great save and knocked the ball over the bar.

Even though both teams had chances to score and take the lead, they were wasteful in front of goal.

The story was no different in extra time. Milan had a golden chance to win the game, but the player tried to control the ball rather than just kick it into an open goal six yards away – allowing Juventus to clear it away. Finally, Juventus had a goal disallowed for offside before the game finished at 1-1. The winner would have to be decided by a nerve-wracking penalty shoot-out.

★ GIANLUIGI DONNARUMMA ★

Although many of the players were dreading the penalty shoot-out, Gianluigi tried his best to stay calm. He had already gotten a reputation for being a good penalty stopper, despite only being halfway through his first full season.

The shoot-out got off to the worst possible start for Milan. Juventus were the first to kick, and midfielder Claudio Marchisio was able to start the scoring after sending Gianluigi the wrong way.

Milan's Gianluca Lapadula tried to get his team off to an equally positive start, but his attempt was easily saved.

★ FOOTBALL RISING STARS ★

But all hope was not lost just yet. Juventus missed their next penalty, the ball flying well over the bar, and both teams scored their next two attempts to level the score at 3-3.

Juventus player Paulo Dybala stepped up to take the fifth penalty for his club. In goal, Gianluigi spread his arms out, his six-foot-five frame seeming to fill the space. Dybala stepped back and took a long run-up, then hit the ball hard and high to the right. Gianluigi guessed which way to dive correctly

and, although the ball was high, was able to reach up and push it away.

Milan just needed to score the next penalty to win ...

Mario Pašalić walked up to the spot. After carefully placing the ball on the ground and taking a few steps back, he ran up and blasted it into the top left-hand corner.

Milan had won the Supercoppa Italiana! And, of course, Gianluigi's save had helped them do it. The team had got their revenge for the Coppa Italia final defeat, and Gianluigi had won the first piece of silverware of his career.

Despite the optimism before the season began and the Supercoppa victory, Milan had yet another average season by their usual high standards. The highest they reached in the league was third place, before spending the rest of the season between fifth and seventh.

Gianluigi played in every single game over the season, keeping a total of twelve clean sheets in forty-one games.

★ **GIANLUIGI DONNARUMMA** ★

Milan finished sixth at the end of the season, which was just enough to allow them to play in the third qualification round for the Europa League. It would be their first entry into a European competition for a few years.

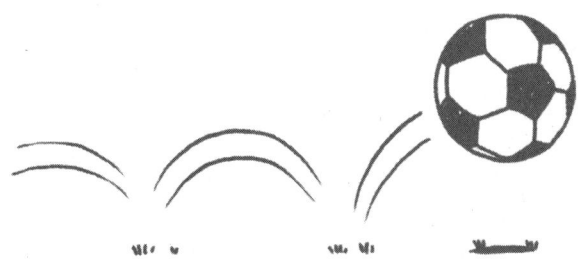

6
MONEY TALKS

The end of the season also began a series of events that would cause a difficult relationship between Gianluigi and AC Milan, ultimately leading to a rather messy break-up years later.

Milan had been quick to offer the

★ GIANLUIGI DONNARUMMA ★

young keeper a new contract as soon as they were able to, wanting to tie him down to the club so that they didn't lose a potential world-class player for little money.

The barrier stopping Milan from getting what they wanted in the contract talks was the old nemesis of all football clubs: the player's agent.

Gianluigi's agent was Mino Raiola, who had a client list including some of the best players in the world: Zlatan Ibrahimović, Paul Pogba and Erling Haaland.

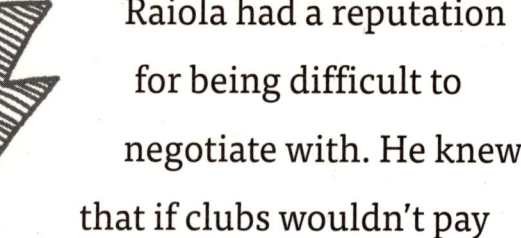

Raiola had a reputation for being difficult to negotiate with. He knew that if clubs wouldn't pay what he considered his clients were worth, there were plenty of other clubs that would.

When he outright rejected Milan's offer to Gianluigi, which was rumoured to be worth over €4 million a year, clubs across Europe were put on alert. It was said that the agreement was being held up by Raiola's request for a release clause that would make it easier for

★ **GIANLUIGI DONNARUMMA** ★

Gianluigi to leave Milan, if the club failed to qualify for the Champions League in the future. Eventually, the Milan chairman announced that Gianluigi had decided not to accept any contract offer.

The whole thing left a bitter taste in the mouths of not just AC Milan fans, but also in the mouths of Italian fans in general.

During Italy's under 21s European Championship group stage game against Denmark, Gianluigi was bombarded with boos. Fake banknotes rained down from the stands into the goal, causing the game to be suspended for a short time.

Either the hard approach from his agent or the backlash from the fans led to Gianluigi accepting a new contract with AC Milan.

The four-year deal was worth over €5 million a year and included an agreement on a return to the club for Gianluigi's older brother Antonio, who had been transferred out of the club. There's a reason right there to be nice to your siblings – it could lead to a well-paid job for you one day!

★ GIANLUIGI DONNARUMMA ★

Knowing that he was no longer popular amongst the AC Milan fans, Gianluigi decided to show them that he was worth the money. But more importantly, he also decided to show them that he was worthy of their trust and of the club.

THE TWO GIANLUIGIS

Everyone has their sporting heroes, and the professionals are no exception. Very few people get to actually meet their heroes, let alone be part of the same team as them.

As a youngster, Gianluigi had posters of his favourite players all

★ GIANLUIGI DONNARUMMA ★

over his bedroom walls. One in particular was someone he shared a first name with: Gianluigi Buffon.

Buffon is considered to be one of the greatest goalkeepers of all time. He made his international debut in 1997, a whole sixteen months before Gianluigi was even born! His career lasted twenty-eight years, and he made over 1,000 appearances for club and country in that time. He won everything there was to win, from league titles to the World Cup. The only competition

he was never able to win was the Champions League, where he was a runner up with Juventus an agonising three times. Not only did Buffon win numerous trophies, but he also won many goalkeeping awards.

Gianluigi's performances in his debut season at Milan had already drawn comparisons with Buffon, and there was talk of Gianluigi being the 'heir' to the Italian goalkeeping role.

He had already represented Italy at youth level, playing for the U17s and

U21s teams. Aged just seventeen, he became the youngest player to ever play for the U21s side.

Many people thought that Gianluigi would be picked for Italy's 2016 Euros squad, but unfortunately he wasn't selected.

However, the young goalkeeper wouldn't have to wait long to make an appearance for Italy's first team.

On the 27th of August 2016, he was selected by the new Italy manager Gian Ventura to be part of the international first team squad for a friendly against France, as well as a World Cup qualifying game. Also in the squad was the current Italy number one – Buffon.

As part of his youth team responsibilities at Milan, Gianluigi was a ball boy at home games. Whenever Milan played against Juventus, Gianluigi always stayed behind the away team's goal so that he could watch and learn from Buffon.

Now as an international teammate of his idol, he had the chance to train and learn from him directly. Buffon was an admirer of Gianluigi, calling

★ GIANLUIGI DONNARUMMA ★

 him extraordinary and the most likely goalkeeper to follow and replace him.

In the friendly against France, the torch was passed at half-time when Gianluigi came on to replace Buffon. By making his debut, Gianluigi became the youngest ever Italian international player to be selected, aged just seventeen years and six months old (a record previously held by … Buffon).

Fearless as ever, Gianluigi didn't look at all nervous. As the two teams came back onto the pitch, he even shared a joke with French midfielder Paul Pogba.

Italy was already 2-1 down, and they would have been further behind if not for a couple of good saves from Gianluigi – including a Pogba free kick that went through the defensive wall, bouncing awkwardly in front of a full-length dive by Gianluigi. Luckily, he caught the ball and held onto it.

After that, Gianluigi became a regular in the Italy squad. He made his first starting appearance in March

★ GIANLUIGI DONNARUMMA ★

2017, against the Netherlands in a 1-2 away win. With this appearance, aged eighteen years and thirty-one days old, he became the youngest goalkeeper to start for Italy.

By this point, Gianluigi was now widely considered to be the natural replacement for Buffon, who was rumoured to be ready to retire from international football.

Unfortunately, Italy failed to qualify for the 2018 World Cup.

Buffon had planned on retiring from international football after the tournament. But now that Italy wouldn't be playing in it, he tearfully made the announcement at the end of the final qualifying game instead. He made one final appearance in a friendly a few months later, partly in tribute to a former teammate who had recently died. At the end of his career, Buffon was officially Italy's most-capped player with 176 appearances.

Gianluigi immediately became the first-choice goalkeeper for Italy following Buffon's retirement. He played in every match of Italy's UEFA

★ GIANLUIGI DONNARUMMA ★

Nations League tournament, only missing Euros qualifying matches through injury.

At the age of forty-three, Buffon returned to his first club – Parma. His drive and determination to keep playing massively inspired Gianluigi.

Gianluigi had already broken Buffon's record of the youngest goalkeeper to make 200 Serie A appearances, and he wondered what else he could do to build a legacy just as impressive as his idol's.

8
A DISAPPOINTING SEASON

AC Milan started the 2017/2018 season with their Europa League qualifying matches against Romanian side Universitatea Craiova. Gianluigi kept a clean sheet in both games,

GIANLUIGI DONNARUMMA

helping Milan win the first leg 0-1 and the second leg 2-0.

In the play-off round against North Macedonian side Shkëndija, Gianluigi kept two more clean sheets. Milan won the first leg 6-0 and the second leg 0-1.

After the qualifying and play-off games, Milan finally made it into the full Europa League tournament. It was their first European appearance in several years, and they would get the chance to qualify for the Champions League if they won it, so they took the tournament very seriously.

Milan won three and drew two of their group stage games. The final match was the only one Gianluigi did not play in, and it was also the only one Milan lost. But it didn't matter! They had already qualified for the knock-out stage.

Meanwhile in the league, Milan was having another disappointing season, floating between the lower top half to mid-table. On a positive note, Gianluigi did reach a big milestone when he played his hundredth game for Milan in a

★ GIANLUIGI DONNARUMMA ★

1-1 draw with Fiorentina. He was the youngest player to reach one hundred games for Milan. However, what should have been a happy occasion was clouded by more contract drama.

Reports were coming out that his agent was trying to get the contract Gianluigi signed in the summer cancelled through various legal loopholes. If he succeeded, that meant Gianluigi could leave the club as a free agent and sign for another club in January.

The Milan fans reacted furiously, even making a banner telling Gianluigi

★ **FOOTBALL RISING STARS** ★

to leave their club. A tearful Gianluigi took to social media to try to defuse the situation, but the whole thing affected him so much that even his form suffered.

Despite all the talk and anger, nothing changed and Gianluigi continued as Milan's first-choice keeper.

After beating Lazio 5-4 on penalties, Milan made it into the Coppa Italia final. Gianluigi was extremely instrumental in that victory, saving two of Lazio's shots. Unfortunately, the team would go on to lose the final 4-0 to Juventus.

Milan also eased into the round of 16 in the Europa League, winning 0-3 and 1-0 over two legs against Bulgarian side Ludogorets.

The Milan players had yet to face a real challenge in the Europa League, having swept aside every team they'd come up against in the qualifying and play-off rounds. Apart from one tricky group stage game, they had made it to the knock-out stages with relative ease.

Gianluigi had played in all but three games, not even in the squad for the two games that didn't matter. He'd kept six clean sheets in nine games, only conceding four goals in total by that point. Regardless of the quality of the opposition, his job was still to keep the ball out of the net – which he did.

However, everything changed for Milan and Gianluigi in the round of 16, because they had been drawn against Arsenal.

The first leg was at home at the San Siro stadium. The home crowd

★ GIANLUIGI DONNARUMMA ★

should've been an advantage, but the game didn't get off to the best of starts for Milan.

In the 15th minute, a wicked deflection blasted the ball over Gianluigi's head and into the back of the net, putting Arsenal ahead early in the game. And no matter how hard Milan tried, they just couldn't find a response.

On the stroke of half-time, matters got even worse. A through ball cut Milan's defence in two, and Arsenal's Aaron Ramsey cleverly wrong-footed Gianluigi and scored to make it 0-2.

No more goals were scored. Arsenal could have won by four or five more, if not for bad finishing and Gianluigi making saves – including a last-ditch head first dive at the feet of Danny Welbeck.

For the second leg, Milan travelled to the Emirates Stadium in North London. They needed to win the match by at least three goals to progress in the competition. It would be difficult, but the players were determined to try. Gianluigi did his part early on by keeping Arsenal from scoring, then his teammates came together and managed to score the opening goal. In the 35th minute, Turkish midfielder Hakan Çalhanoğlu's sublime thirty-yard effort found the back of the net. Milan were winning 0-1!

However, the celebrations didn't last long.

A few minutes later, Welbeck was nudged in the Milan box and fell over when the ball went out of play, winning a penalty for Arsenal. Although Welbeck did seem to fall a little too dramatically, Gianluigi's questioning of the decision earned him a yellow card. Arsenal scored the resulting penalty to put the game back in their favour.

Two more goals from Arsenal sealed Milan's fate. One goal came from a wicked bounce off Gianluigi as the ball moved in the air, and the other one came from a follow-up to a save.

Milan were out of the competition … again. The Europa League is the one European championship Milan have never won, but the team would

✭ GIANLUIGI DONNARUMMA ✭

soon get another chance. Finishing sixth in Serie A meant they qualified for the tournament next season, so their hopes of someday winning the competition were very much kept alive.

9
GOODBYE, MILAN

The following seasons saw steady progress for Gianluigi and Milan.

In February 2019, after making five key saves to stop a defeat, Gianluigi earned his first Man of the Match award in a 1-1 draw with Roma. That same month, he also made his 150th appearance for the club. Throughout the 2018/2019 season, Gianluigi shared goalkeeping duties with Pepe Reina. The plan was for Reina to play in goal during the Europa League, while Gianluigi started in Serie A. Although Milan failed to qualify from the group stage of the Europa League, they were able to finish fifth in the league.

However, the club broke the financial fair play rules (which are supposed to stop clubs spending more than they earn) and were banned from

★ FOOTBALL RISING STARS ★

competing in Europe the following season.

In the 2019/2020 season, Gianluigi made his 200th appearance for Milan in a 1-2 victory over Sassuolo, just like his debut. This game also saw another milestone for Gianluigi. When captain Alessio Romagnoli was substituted with injury, the armband was passed to Gianluigi – making him captain for the first time.

The 2020/2021 season was Gianluigi's best season at Milan. He was the starting

★ GIANLUIGI DONNARUMMA ★

goalkeeper and also the occasional captain. Fourteen clean sheets in thirty-seven games and a 71% save percentage helped Milan to a second-place league finish. Gianluigi also won the Goalkeeper of the Year award and a place in the Serie A Team of the Year.

That season also saw the start of a familiar debate: would Gianluigi sign a new contract? With Gianluigi's contract ending at the end of the season, an improving Milan were once again eager to sign him up to a new one, but once again they would have to deal with his agent.

Agents have all sorts of tricks, and one of them involves telling a friendly journalist that their client is in talks with another club. When it is then reported that a club is interested in the player and prepared to pay whatever, the player's current club are more likely to up their offer to hold onto them. Using this trick often means the player wants to leave, and the speculation starts a bidding war – increasing the player's new wage offer significantly.

★ GIANLUIGI DONNARUMMA ★

Agents with valuable clients make a lot of money from new contracts and transfers, so there is a very high possibility that many rumours and arguments about these things are started by the player's agent. It is a horrible side of the game where personal financial gain is more important than anything else. For example, it was reported that Gianluigi's agent wanted to earn €20 million if Gianluigi signed a new contract with Milan.

At a time when Gianluigi was reportedly the third highest-paid goalkeeper in the world, Milan were struggling a little with money. Gianluigi's agent, Raiola, was still playing hardball and had rejected a generous offer – one that would have also seen him get a very large bonus.

With more stories coming out about other clubs talking to Gianluigi, Milan called his bluff, rejected all terms and even went out and signed a new goalkeeper.

Besides the fight over his salary, there were other reasons Gianluigi

GIANLUIGI DONNARUMMA

might have wanted to leave Milan. Not only had the club been struggling for a long time, but they also lacked stability. Throughout his time there, Gianluigi had seen three different owners, five changes of manager and numerous different coaches join and leave the club. Plus, the chance to go somewhere with a real chance of adding trophies to his career must have appealed just as much as an increased salary.

And so, in May 2021, it was finally confirmed that Gianluigi would leave Milan when his contract expired at the end of June.

★ **FOOTBALL RISING STARS** ★

Many people thought it seemed like an odd time for Gianluigi to leave, as things were actually on the up for Milan. Their second-place finish in Serie A meant they were back in the Champions League and in contention for domestic glory.

Gianluigi had made 251 appearances in total for the club and kept eighty-eight clean sheets, but now it was time to start somewhere new.

Where Gianluigi would go exactly was up in the air now that he was leaving. His agent's attempts to increase his wages even more meant some clubs just couldn't afford him. Juventus and Barcelona in particular were possible choices, but their finances were too low. Although it was uncertain who he would be playing in goal for next season, the one certainty was that it wouldn't be for Milan.

But before Gianluigi could make an impact with another club, he would be joining his Italian teammates for the biggest international competition of his life so far: Euro 2020.

10
ROAD TO THE FINAL

Italy qualified for the 2020 Euros with a 100% record. Winning all ten qualification games, the team scored thirty-seven goals and only conceded four in the process. Gianluigi played in five matches. He missed three through injury and stayed on the

GIANLUIGI DONNARUMMA

bench for the others, as Italy manager Roberto Mancini rotated the squad in the 'easier' games.

The tournament was to be played across several countries instead of the usual format of just one or two countries hosting, and Italy had been selected as a host nation. Due to the COVID-19 pandemic, the tournament was delayed by a year and took place in the summer of 2021 instead.

Gianluigi was Italy's first-choice goalkeeper going into the Euros, having made twenty-six appearances before the tournament.

Italy were drawn in Group A with Turkey, Switzerland and Wales, and the team continued their impressive form with three wins in front of their own fans in Roma's Stadio Olimpico. Gianluigi also kept three clean sheets, as they won 3-0, 3-0 and 1-0. Advancing to the round of 16, Italy faced Austria in a game played at Wembley Stadium in London. It was a fairly quiet game, with Italy having the better of the rare chances that came along.

★ GIANLUIGI DONNARUMMA ★

In the second half, a close-range header by Austria's Marko Arnautović went into the goal off the bar. Arnautović celebrated by running over to the Italy fans and shushing them … only for the goal to be ruled out for offside by VAR.

Full time ended at 0-0, so the game went into extra time.

Italy finally took the lead in the 95th minute, then doubled it ten minutes later to make it 2-0. A place in the quarter-final was within touching distance!

Austria nearly got back into the

game with a thunderous left-foot shot that was destined for the goal, before Gianluigi dived to the ground and knocked the ball away with a strong hand.

As Italy pulled back to hold onto the lead, Austria pushed forward. Austria managed to score a scrambled goal from a corner, but Italy held on to win 2-1.

For the quarter-final, Italy headed to the Allianz Arena in Germany to face Belgium. Gianluigi made two world-class saves after attempts by Kevin De Bruyne and Romelu Lukaku, before Italy's Nicolò Barella scored in the 31st minute to make it 1-0. Lorenzo Insigne then gave Italy a 2-0 advantage with a stunning curling shot from outside of the box. Injury time in the first half saw Belgium get a penalty, and Lukaku sent Gianluigi the wrong way to make it 2-1.

Belgium dominated and had chances in the second half, but they wasted them all. Italy won the game, setting up a semi-final against Spain.

The first half of the semi-final was

closely contested, with both Italy and Spain having chances. No goals were scored until the 60th minute, when Federico Chiesa put Italy in the lead.

Seeing Álvaro Morata warming up and then coming on as a late substitute would have given Gianluigi flashbacks to the Coppa Italia final in 2016, all the way back in his debut season. Morata scored the winning goal that night, and

Gianluigi was likely hoping that history wasn't about to repeat itself.

The final was in sight,

★ **GIANLUIGI DONNARUMMA** ★

until Gianluigi's fear came true. Spain scored ... And it was Morata with the goal, wrong-footing Gianluigi in the process.

It was 1-1 at full time, so the game went into extra time. Morata could have scored again, but Gianluigi got to the ball first and punched it away.

With the score still level by the end of extra time, the game went to penalties.

Gianluigi's penalty-saving skills had yet to turn up this tournament, so it was a big moment for him. Both teams missed their first penalties but scored their next two. Italy's Federico Bernardeschi then scored his penalty to make it 3-2 in the shoot-out.

Gianluigi moved into position in goal and looked up to see who would be taking Spain's must-score next penalty.

It was Álvero Morata.

Gianluigi stood still on the line as Morata began his run-up. Just as Morata kicked the ball, Gianluigi sprang into action, diving to his left. The penalty was low, but Gianluigi reached down and saved it!

★ **GIANLUIGI DONNARUMMA** ★

This was his revenge for the Coppa Italia final all those years ago.

Italy scored the deciding penalty and went through to the final!

11
PENALTIES

Penalty shoot-outs. No one likes them. Even when a team wins one, it can feel a bit underwhelming. Penalties were brought into the game to break the cycle of endless replays in cup competitions, and it is difficult to come up with an alternative way to

GIANLUIGI DONNARUMMA

settle a game. Some teams even play for penalties, especially if it doesn't look like they'll win the game.

England and Italy both have unhappy memories of penalty shoot-outs. England have only won two out of nine shoot-outs in major tournament finals, while Italy have lost six and won five. When both teams reached the final of the 2020 Euros, they each hoped to avoid going to the dreaded penalties.

On the 11th of July 2021, during a warm summer night in London, the final took place at Wembley Stadium.

★ **FOOTBALL RISING STARS** ★

England had the home advantage in front of over 60,000 fans, and it was England that started the brightest.

In the 2nd minute, Luke Shaw half-volleyed a Kieran Trippier cross past a stranded Gianluigi. The ball was in the net before he could react. England continued to dominate possession without really threatening Italy for most of the first half.

Italy started to come back into the game in the second half, creating chance after chance. They finally scored when a half-cleared corner was scrambled home by defender

✦ GIANLUIGI DONNARUMMA ✦

Leonardo Bonucci to make it 1-1.

Italy continued to attack, looking for a winner. The rest of the game mostly took place in England's half, so Gianluigi was a spectator in Italy's goal.

Neither team could break the deadlock after ninety minutes. Italy pushed for the winning goal in extra time but couldn't score. The final had to be decided by penalties.

By that point, Gianluigi had a history of taking part in the dreaded shoot-outs. He had a

 perfect record in them, winning all four he had been a part of over his career – three for AC Milan and one for Italy in the semi-final against Spain.

Yet again, the pressure was on Gianluigi to help see Italy through.

Italy won the coin toss and chose to shoot first. Domenico Berardi got his team off to a good start and scored his penalty.

England's first penalty taker was captain Harry Kane. Gianluigi guessed which way to go correctly,

★ GIANLUIGI DONNARUMMA ★

diving to his right, but Kane's penalty was too good and the score was levelled at 1-1.

Italy missed their second attempt, while Harry Maguire sent Gianluigi the wrong way with his penalty. He blasted the ball into the top corner, putting England in control at 1-2.

Bonucci scored to make it 2-2, and then Marcus Rashford stepped up to the spot. Taking a wide run up, he shuffled and paused before kicking the ball. Gianluigi went the wrong way, but luckily

the ball hit the post. Italy scored their next penalty to take back the lead and make it 3-2.

The tension ramped up in the stadium. England needed to score, and the responsibility was on Jordan Sancho. He took a short run-up, but his penalty was at a good height for Gianluigi, who dived to his left and saved it.

Italy just needed to score to win … but England were given a lifeline. Jordan Pickford saved Italy's fifth penalty, turning the ball onto the post.

★ GIANLUIGI DONNARUMMA ★

Bukayo Saka had to score to send the shoot-out into sudden death. He did a quick run on the spot before taking his shot. Before Saka had even kicked the ball, Gianluigi started his dive, going to his left. Again, the penalty wasn't a good one. It was too close to the goalkeeper and at a good height, making it an easy save for Gianluigi.

With Gianluigi making two vital saves in the shoot-out, Italy won! They were European champions!

And yet, Gianluigi didn't react. He walked away from the goal, as cool as ice. He didn't celebrate saving Saka's penalty, as he was just focussed on the *next* penalty he had to face. It wasn't until he looked towards the halfway line and saw his teammates running towards him that he realised what had happened. The moment didn't get a chance to sink in, as he was jumped on and crowded by his team screaming in joy.

For his performances throughout the competition, including keeping three clean sheets, making nine saves and conceding only four goals in seven appearances, he was

GIANLUIGI DONNARUMMA

named Player of the Tournament by UEFA. It was the first time a goalkeeper had ever won the award.

After the Euros, Gianluigi's life changed dramatically. Further recognition of his success came when he won the Yashin trophy – named after Lev Yashin, who was the only goalkeeper to ever win the Ballon d'Or. Italy also gave Gianluigi one of the country's highest honours for his services to Italian sport: the Order of Merit of the Italian Republic.

★ FOOTBALL RISING STARS ★

To cap off a great year for Gianluigi, he led the Italian national team out as captain in a Nations League game against Belgium. He was the youngest captain since 1965 and helped the team to a 2-1 victory. He almost kept a clean sheet, having made two great saves to deny Belgium before they scored a consolation goal very late in the game.

12
A NEW START

Just days after the 2020 Euros final, Gianluigi officially signed for top French club Paris Saint-Germain (PSG).

Juventus came close to signing Gianluigi, but that all changed when their new manager came in and decided that he preferred the club's current goalkeeper. Barcelona were also hovering, but they already had one of the best goalkeepers in the world: Marc-André ter Stegen.

PSG had supposedly dropped out of the running early when they extended the contract of their current goalkeeper, Chile international Keylor Navas, but this was still when Gianluigi and Milan were deep in talks and a decision had yet to be made.

Navas was thirty-four years old at the time, and although a goalkeeper's

★ GIANLUIGI DONNARUMMA ★

career tends to be longer than other players', he would need a suitable replacement sooner rather than later. And luckily for Gianluigi, PSG thought that replacement could be him.

As one of the richest clubs in the world, the demands being made by Gianluigi's agent weren't an issue for PSG – unlike Juventus, whose early offer was outbid by PSG. Gianluigi signed a five-year contract worth a reported €10 million a year, and his agent obviously got his share too …

In addition to Gianluigi, other notable signings PSG made that summer included the experienced Spanish defender Sergio Ramos, Dutch midfielder Georginio Wijnaldum and world-class forward Lionel Messi. All three players were signed on a free transfer, which is a good job really because Messi's wages alone would've been unbelievably expensive.

By adding these incredible players to their side, it was clear that PSG were making a statement about their continued pursuit of Champions League victory. The club were determined to win, and now they had added some big names to their already

★ GIANLUIGI DONNARUMMA ★

impressive squad of players to help them do it.

In the 2021/2022 season, PSG dominated Ligue 1 (the French first division). They topped the table after their third game and stayed there, easily winning with eighty-six points. Marseille, their biggest rivals, finished second with seventy-one points – that's a huge difference of fifteen points!

It is not unfair to suggest that PSG could probably put a traffic cone in goal and still win the league, given the pool of talented players in their squad compared to the rest of the league, but that doesn't make the role of goalkeeper any less important.

Gianluigi shared goalkeeping duties with Navas throughout the season, only playing in seventeen league matches due to injury. He also missed a few games because he had the COVID-19 virus.

In a total of twenty-four games played across all competitions, Gianluigi kept nine clean sheets.

Five of those appearances were in the Champions League, which was the real focus of PSG. Gianluigi played in three of the six group games, even managing to keep a clean sheet in his Champions League debut in a 2-0 victory over Manchester City.

Finishing second in the group stage set PSG up with a very tricky knock-out round against Real Madrid.

The first leg was at home in a packed Parc des Princes stadium in Paris. Real Madrid's Thibaut Courtois was the busier of the two goalkeepers during the match – even saving a Lionel Messi penalty. It took a moment of

★★ FOOTBALL RISING STARS ★★

 individual skill from Kylian Mbappé to break the deadlock well into injury time, giving PSG a 1-0 victory and the upper hand for the second leg.

Three weeks later at Real Madrid's home ground, Santiago Bernabéu, PSG scored near the end of the first half. This made their total score for the two legs 2-0 so far. It would take something special for Real Madrid to come back into this one.

Unfortunately for PSG, something special came in the shape of Real Madrid striker Karim Benzema.

★ GIANLUIGI DONNARUMMA ★

In the second half of the game, Benzema scored a hat-trick within an unbelievable seventeen minutes.

The first goal sadly came from a Gianluigi mistake, after he gave the ball away when put under high pressure. For the other two goals, there was not much he could have done to save them. The second took a nasty deflection, and the winning goal was a tidy first-time finish right in the corner of the net.

PSG were out of the Champions League.

There was further cup upset for Gianluigi in the Coupe de France round of 16 tie against Nice, when he had to face yet another penalty shoot-out.

Despite being agonisingly close to saving two penalties, he did manage to save one – diving at full length to his right to beat the ball away. But it wasn't enough. PSG missed two penalties and lost the shoot-out 6-5.

It was a disappointing end to Gianluigi's first season.

13
DOMESTIC GLORY

Gianluigi's second season at PSG was a much more consistent one. He became the first-choice goalkeeper and kept his place throughout nearly all of the season, only missing two early rounds of cup ties.

PSG started the 2022/2023 season

with a 0-5 win against Clermont Foot, putting them at the top of the table. Gianluigi only faced one shot all match, which he saved well.

The coming weeks gave him a lot more to do, as he made many crucial saves in the following games. He was named Man of the Match for his performance against Toulouse, saving all seven shots that came his way. His performances helped PSG to an unbeaten start of sixteen games.

That's not to say it was an easy ride

GIANLUIGI DONNARUMMA

for them. RC Lens and Marseille were nipping at their heels the whole way through the campaign. Marseille fell away a little, but it was a 3-1 victory over RC Lens towards the end of the season that gave PSG some space.

PSG finished the season as champions with eighty-five points, and RC Lens finished just one point behind them.

The tale of Gianluigi's individual season was of his usual high standards. Playing in all but ten minutes of the league, he was on the pitch for a total of 3,410 minutes!

He achieved a huge 76% save percentage, saving 124 out of 164 shots, and kept thirteen clean sheets in thirty-eight games.

Further success came from a victory in the 2022 French Super Cup (known as the Trophée des Champions), a game between the previous season's Ligue 1 and Coupe de France winners. PSG easily beat Nantes 4-0 to claim their eleventh Super Cup.

However, PSG's story of success was about to come to a disappointing end. The Coupe de France title was

★ GIANLUIGI DONNARUMMA ★

not to be theirs, after they crashed out in the round of 16 to rivals Marseille.

More European heartbreak for Gianluigi came in the Champions League, as PSG lost to Bayern Munich in the knock-out stages.

During the 2023/2024 season, fate conspired to put AC Milan and PSG in the same Champions League group. Then, on the 25th of October 2023, exactly eight years to the day Gianluigi had made his professional debut for Milan, the two teams were set to play against each other.

It was the first time Gianluigi had faced his former club since leaving. A 3-0 victory and a clean sheet for his team may have felt bittersweet, but it was something to be proud of.

PSG and Milan's second group game saw Gianluigi return to the San Siro stadium in Italy. It was an uncomfortable night, with a hostile reception from the Milan fans as they once again threw fake banknotes at him. In the highly-charged atmosphere, Milan won 2-1, but PSG qualified above them in the group on goal difference.

★ GIANLUIGI DONNARUMMA ★

Gianluigi's move to PSG had bought him some winner's medals, and the quality of the club promised that there was so much more to come. With a reliable European champion in their goal, anything seemed possible.

14
WHAT'S NEXT?

The 2023/2024 season was full of mixed emotions for Gianluigi and PSG.

In January 2024, Gianluigi helped his team win the delayed 2023 Trophée des Champions game 2-0! It was a huge moment and a great start to the year.

GIANLUIGI DONNARUMMA

PSG made it to the semi-finals of the Champions League, but Borussia Dortmund put up a fight and knocked them out of the competition. This disappointment didn't last long, though. With Gianluigi standing strong in goal, PSG beat Lyon 2-1 in the Coupe de France final! PSG's trophy cabinet only got fuller when they wrapped up yet another Ligue 1 title.

After the season was over, Gianluigi joined up with his Italy teammates for the 2024 Euros in Germany. Not only were the team defending their title, but they also had something to prove.

★ FOOTBALL RISING STARS ★

Despite their 2020 Euros victory, Italy had failed to qualify for the 2022 World Cup – and it had been a huge embarrassment.

Although they didn't lose a game in their World Cup qualifying group and only conceded two goals, they drew too many games and finished in second place. To qualify, they needed to win in a play-off, which they lost 1-0 against North Macedonia. The finger of blame pointed at Gianluigi, but Italy's real problems lay at the other end of the pitch.

The 2024 Euros was Italy's chance

to prove that they could still perform well, but being the previous winners meant that there was a lot of pressure on the team.

After making it through the group stage with a win, loss and draw, Italy faced Switzerland in the round of 16. The match was hard to watch, as Italy really struggled to find opportunities to score. In a disappointing turn of events, Switzerland went on to win 2-0 and Italy were knocked out of Euro 2024. It was a disaster!

As the captain of the team, Gianluigi spoke honestly about where they had gone wrong and apologised to the Italy fans. 'I realise it is tough to accept these words right now,' he said, 'but we have to look to the future.'

Even though Italy are no longer the current European champions, Gianluigi is still one of the best goalkeepers in the world. Regardless of how some places in Italy feel about him, he has achieved great things in football at such a young age. When a goalkeeper's career can last until they are forty, this rising star may continue to rise for a good long while yet.